OH, WHAT AN
Awful THING
TO SAY!

OH, WHAT AN *Awful* THING TO SAY!

*Needles, Skewers, Pricks,
and Outright Nastiness*

COMPILED BY
WILLIAM COLE AND
LOUIS PHILLIPS

ST. MARTIN'S PRESS • NEW YORK

NOTE TO THE READER
BOXED QUOTATIONS ARE
"CLASSIC" ZINGERS.

OH, WHAT AN AWFUL THING TO SAY! NEEDLES,
SKEWERS, PRICKS, AND OUTRIGHT NASTINESS.
Copyright © 1991 by William R. Cole and Louis
Phillips. All rights reserved. Printed in the United
States of America. No part of this book may be used
or reproduced in any manner whatsoever without
written permission except in the case of brief quo-
tations embodied in critical articles or reviews. For
information, address St. Martin's Press, 175 Fifth
Avenue, New York, N.Y. 10010

Production Editor: David Stanford Burr

Design by Judy Dannecker

Library of Congress Cataloging-in-Publication Data

Oh, what an awful thing to say! / gathered by
    William Cole and Louis Phillips.
             p.   cm.
        "A Thomas Dunne book."
        ISBN 0-312-07048-9
        1. Invective—Humor.   I. Cole,
    William.   II. Phillips, Louis.
    PN6231.I65037   1992
    82—dc20   91-34807
                                    CIP

First Edition: January 1992

10 9 8 7 6 5 4 3 2 1

> If you can't say anything good about someone, sit right here by me.
> —ALICE ROOSEVELT LONGWORTH

I am free of all prejudices. I hate everyone equally.
—W. C. FIELDS

That's the point of quotations, you know; you can use another's words to be insulting.
"AMANDA CROSS"

. . . Power tends to corrupt, and absolute power corrupts absolutely. Great men are almost always bad.
—LORD ACTON

OH, WHAT AN *Awful* THING TO SAY!

JOHN ADAMS

It has been the political career of this man to begin with hypocrisy, proceed with arrogance, and finish with contempt.

—THOMAS PAINE

JOHN QUINCY ADAMS

It is said he is a disgusting man to do business with. Coarse and dirty and clownish in his address and stiff and abstracted in his opinions, which are drawn from books exclusively.

—WILLIAM HENRY HARRISON

SPIRO AGNEW

Agnew reminds me of the kind of guy who would make a crank call to the Russians on the hot line.

—DICK GREGORY

MUHAMMAD ALI

He floats like an anchor, stings like a moth.

—RAY GANDOLF, TV COMMENTATOR
(on Ali at thirty-nine)

MICHAEL ARLEN

Arlen, for all his reputation, is not a bounder. He is every other inch a gentleman.

—ALEXANDER WOOLLCOTT

MARGOT ASQUITH
The affair between Margot Asquith and Margot
Asquith will live as one of the prettiest love scenes
in all literature.

—DOROTHY PARKER

Lady Astor

Nannie was a devout Christian Scientist, but not a good one. She kept confusing herself with God.

—Mrs. Gordon Smith

Lady Astor and Winston Churchill
Lady Astor: Winston, if I were married to you, I'd put poison in your coffee.
Churchill: Nancy, if you were my wife, I'd drink it.

Clement Attlee

He brings to the fierce struggle of politics the tepid enthusiasm of a lazy summer afternoon at a cricket match.

—Aneurin Bevan

He is a sheep in sheep's clothing.

—Winston Churchill

Charisma? He did not recognize the word except as a clue in his beloved *Times* crossword.

—James Margach

. . . reminds me of nothing so much as a dead fish before it has time to stiffen.

—GEORGE ORWELL

W. H. AUDEN

He is all ice and wooden-faced acrobatics.
—PERCY WYNDHAM LEWIS

JANE AUSTEN

To me, Poe's prose is unreadable—like Jane Austen's. No, there is a difference. I could read his prose on a salary, but not Jane's.

—MARK TWAIN

JAMES BALDWIN

. . . a hustler who comes on like Job.

—ISHMAEL REED

STANLEY BALDWIN

Not even a public figure. A man of no experience. And of the utmost insignificance.

—LORD CURZON

One could not even dignify him with the name of stuffed shirt. He was simply a hole in the air.

—GEORGE ORWELL

ARTHUR BALFOUR, First Lord of the Admiralty

I was playing golf that day
  When the Germans landed.
All our soldiers ran away,
  All our ships were stranded.
Such were my surprise and shame
  They almost put me off my game.
          —ANONYMOUS

Balinger

Mrs. Balinger is one of those ladies who pursue Culture
in bands, as though it were dangerous to meet it alone.
—Edith Wharton

Honoré de Balzac

A fat little flabby person with the face of a baker, the
clothes of a cobbler, the size of a barrelmaker, the manners of a stocking salesman, and the dress of an inn-
keeper.

—Victor de Balabin

Tallulah Bankhead
A day away from Tallulah is like a month in the
country.

—Howard Dietz (attrib.)

The Beatles

. . . bad-mannered little shits.

—Noël Coward

The Beatles are not merely awful; I would consider it
sacrilegious to say anything less than that they are god-
awful. . . . They are so unbelievably horrible, so appall-
ingly unmusical, so dogmatically insensitive to the magic

of the art, that they qualify as crowned heads of anti-music. . . .

—WILLIAM F. BUCKLEY, JR.

CECIL BEATON

His baroque is worse than his bite.

—HANK BRENNAN

Max Beerbohm

It always makes me cross when Max is called "the incomparable Max." He is not incomparable at all. . . . He is a shallow, affected, self-conscious fribble—so there.
—Vita Sackville-West

Ludwig van Beethoven

Beethoven always sounds to me like the upsetting of bags of nails, with here and there an also dropped hammer.
—John Ruskin

Hilaire Belloc and G. K. Chesterton

Two buttocks of one bum.

—T. Sturge Moore

Robert Benchley

Robert Benchley has a style that is weak and lies down frequently to rest.

—Max Eastman

Arnold Bennett

The Hitler of the book-racket.

—Percy Wyndham Lewis

Jack Benny

When Jack Benny plays the violin, it sounds as if the strings are still back in the cat.

—Fred Allen

ALBAN BERG

It is my private opinion that Mr. Berg is just a bluff. But even if he isn't, it is impossible to deny that his music (?) is a soporific, by the side of which the telephone book is a strong cup of coffee.

—SAMUEL CHOTZINOFF

HECTOR BERLIOZ

Berlioz, musically speaking, is a lunatic; a classical composer only in Paris, the great city of quacks. His music is simply and undisguisedly nonsense.

—ANONYMOUS REVIEWER

ANEURIN BEVAN

He will be as great a curse to this country in peace as he was a squalid nuisance in time of war.

—WINSTON CHURCHILL

He enjoys prophesying the imminent end of the capitalist system and is prepared to play a part, any part, in its burial except that of a mute.

—HAROLD MACMILLAN

ERNEST BEVIN

Ernest Bevin objects to ideas only when other people have them.

—A. J. P. TAYLOR

Ambrose Bierce

Bierce would bury his best friend with a sigh of relief, and express satisfaction that he was done with him.

—Jack London

James G. Blaine

Blaine! Blaine! J. G. Blaine!
Continental Liar from the State of Maine.

—Anonymous campaign slogan

James Boswell

That he was a coxcomb and a bore, weak, vain, pushing, curious, garrulous, was obvious to all who were acquainted with him. That he could not reason, that he had no wit, no humor, no eloquence, is apparent from his writings. . . . Nature had made him a slave and an idolater. His mind resembled those creepers which the botanists call parasites and which can subsist only by clinging round the stems and imbibing the juices of stronger plants.

—Thomas Babington Macaulay

Betsy Braddock
Braddock to Winston Churchill:
Winston, you're drunk.
Churchill's reply:
Bessie, you're ugly, but tomorrow I shall be sober.

JOHANNES BRAHMS

I played over the music of that scoundrel Brahms. What a giftless bastard! It annoys me that this self-inflated mediocrity is hailed as a genius. Why, in comparison with him, Raff is a giant, not to speak of Rubinstein, who after all is a live and important human being, while Brahms is chaotic and absolutely empty and dried-up stuff.

—PETER ILYICH TCHAIKOVSKY

BERTOLT BRECHT

I don't regard Brecht as a man of iron-gray purpose and intellect. I think he is a theatrical whore of the first quality.

—PETER HALL

BRITISH ROYAL FAMILY

What a smug stinking lot my relations are . . . and you've never seen such a seedy worn-out bunch of old hags most of them have become.

—DUKE OF WINDSOR
Letter to Wallace Simpson

CRAIG BROWN, British political reporter

He looked like Dylan Thomas pulled through a hedge backwards.

—BERNARD INGHAM,
Margaret Thatcher's press secretary

Elizabeth Barrett Browning

Mrs. Browning's death is rather a relief to me, I must say. No more Aurora Leigh, thank God! A woman of real genius, I know; but what is the upshot of it all? She and her sex had better mind the kitchen and the children, and perhaps the poor. Except in such things as little novels, they only devote themselves to what men do much better, leaving that which men do worse or not at all.

—Edward Fitzgerald

Robert Browning

I don't think Browning was very good in bed. His wife probably didn't care for him very much. He snored and had fantasies about twelve-year-old girls.

—W. H. Auden

His muse is as much invalid as his wife was *invalide*.

—Oliver St. John Gogarty

William Jennings Bryan

The national tear duct.

—H. L. Mencken

One could drive a prairie schooner through any part of his argument and never scrape against a fact.

—David Houston

We put him to school and he wound up stealing the schoolbooks.

—IGNATIUS DONNELLY

A mouthing, slobbering demagogue whose patriotism is all jawbone.

—THOMAS DIXON (1896)

WILLIAM F. BUCKLEY, JR.

It's great to be with Bill Buckley, because you don't have to think. He takes a position and you automatically take the opposite one and you know you're right.

—JOHN KENNETH GALBRAITH

Looks and sounds not unlike Hitler, but without the charm.

—GORE VIDAL

WILLIAM BURROUGHS

[He resembles] a Vermont farmer who had been married to his wife for sixty years, and the day she dies someone says, "I guess you're going to miss her a lot, Zeke," and he says, "No, never did get to like her much."

—NORMAN MAILER

GEORGE BUSH

The unpleasant sound Bush is emitting, as he traipses from one conservative gathering to another, is a thin, tinny "arf"—the sound of a lapdog.

—GEORGE F. WILL

George Bush is a fake, a fool, and a wimp.

—JULES FEIFFER

GEORGE GORDON, LORD BYRON

In his endeavors to corrupt my mind he has sought to make me smile first at Vice, saying, "There is nothing to which a woman may not be reconciled by repetition or familiarity." There is *no* Vice with which he has not endeavored in this manner to familiarize me.

—ANNABELLA MILBANKE (Lady Byron)

> Mad, bad, and dangerous to know.
> —LADY CAROLINE LAMB

HALL CAINE

Mr. Hall Caine, it is true, aims at the grandiose, but then he writes at the top of his voice. He is so loud that one cannot hear what he says.

—OSCAR WILDE

MARIA CALLAS

When Callas carried a grudge, she planted it, nursed it, fostered it, watered it, and watched it grow to sequoia size.

—HAROLD C. SCHONBERG

TRUMAN CAPOTE

He is a sweetly vicious old lady.

—TENNESSEE WILLIAMS

Truman Capote has made lying an art. A *minor* art.

—GORE VIDAL

THOMAS CARLYLE

The same old sausage, fizzing and sputtering in its own grease.

—HENRY JAMES

It is embarrassing how he harps on his wife's dimensions: brave little heart, noble little creature, indomitable little soul—he only just stops short of "wee cowering crimson-tippit Beastie."

—SYLVIA TOWNSEND WARNER

It was very good of God to let Carlyle and Mrs. Carlyle marry one another and so make only two people miserable instead of four.

—SAMUEL BUTLER

EDWARD CARSON

The Right Honourable Sir Edward Henry Carson, Privy Councillor, Master of Arts of Trinity College, Dublin, LLD (Hon. Causa), Member of Parliament and King's Counsellor, the leader of the Ulster Unionist movement and the starry hero of all the politest young ladies of Belfast, has not done anything to promote the well-being of Ireland, never has done anything, and never will.

—ST. JOHN ERVINE

BILLY CARTER

Jimmy needs Billy like Van Gogh needs stereo.
—JOHNNY CARSON

JIMMY CARTER

I would not want Jimmy Carter and his men put in charge of snake control in Ireland.
—EUGENE MCCARTHY

I think Jimmy Carter as president is like Truman Capote marrying Dolly Parton. The job is just too big for him.
—RICH LITTLE (attrib.)

JIMMY CARTER, GERALD FORD, AND RICHARD M. NIXON

History buffs probably noted the reunion at a Washington party a few weeks ago of three ex-presidents: Carter, Ford, and Nixon—See No Evil, Hear No Evil, and Evil.

—SENATOR ROBERT J. DOLE

VISCOUNT CASTLEREAGH

EPITAPH
Posterity will ne'er survey
A nobler grave than this;
Here lie the bones of Castlereagh:
Stop, traveler, and piss.
—GEORGE GORDON, LORD BYRON

> Why is a pump like V-sc—nt C-st—r—gh?
> Because it is a slender thing of wood,
> That up and down its awkward arm doth sway,
> And coolly spout and spout and spout away,
> In one weak, washy, everlasting flood!
> —THOMAS MOORE

NEVILLE CHAMBERLAIN

Listening to a speech by Chamberlain is like paying a visit to Woolworth's; everything in its place and nothing above sixpence.

—WINSTON CHURCHILL

Neville Chamberlain is no better than a mayor of Birmingham, and in a lean year at that.

—LORD HUGH CECIL

. . . a retail mind in a wholesale business.

—DAVID LLOYD GEORGE

Chamberlain (who has the mind and manner of a clothesbrush) aims only at assuring temporary peace at the price of ultimate defeat.

—SIR HAROLD NICOLSON

PRINCE CHARLES

Prince Charles loves nostalgia—pitched roofs, pastiche, details, Victorian architecture. The institution of mon-

archy is preposterous in a technological society—you can't wear a crown in midtown Manhattan. But if the gentry are in their Palladian houses, the stoical artisans in their pebble-dash houses tugging their forelocks—if you recreate the past, then the institution of the monarchy and class privilege is tenable.

—J. G. BALLARD

King Charles II

Here lies our mutton-loving king,
Whose word no man relies on;
Who never said a foolish thing,
And never did a wise one.
—John Wilmot, Earl of Rochester

Chevy Chase

I said that I didn't think Chevy Chase could ad-lib a fart after a baked bean dinner. I think he took umbrage at that a little bit.

—Johnny Carson

Vicomte Chateaubriand

He thinks himself deaf because he no longer hears himself talked of.

—Charles-Maurice de Talleyrand

G. K. Chesterton

Here lies Mr. Chesterton,
Who to heaven might have gone,
But didn't when he heard the news
That the place was run by Jews.
—Humbert Wolfe

Chesterton is like a vile scum on a pond. . . . All his slop . . .

—Ezra Pound

Poor. G. K. C., his day is past—
Now God will know the truth at last.

—E. V. Lucas

Frédéric Chopin

A composer for the right hand.

—Richard Wagner

Randolph Churchill

A chain drinker.

—Anonymous

Dear Randolph, utterly unspoiled by his great failure.

—Noël Coward

> (Randolph Churchill had entered the hospital and his lung was removed even though it was not malignant.)
> A typical triumph of modern science to find the only part of Randolph that was not malignant and remove it.
>
> —Evelyn Waugh

Winston Churchill

. . . a man suffering from petrified adolescence.

—Aneurin Bevan

. . . he would make a drum out of the skin of his own mother in order to sound his own praises.

—David Lloyd George

I welcome this opportunity of pricking the bloated bladder of lies with the poniard of truth.

—Aneurin Bevan

He refers to a defeat as a disaster as though it came from God, but to a victory as though it came from himself.

—ANEURIN BEVAN

He has spoilt himself by reading about Napoleon.

—DAVID LLOYD GEORGE

If you think I'm gaga, you should see Winston.

—W. SOMERSET MAUGHAM

Winston has devoted the best years of his life to preparing his impromptu speeches.

—FREDERICK EDWIN SMITH

Simply a radio personality who outlived his prime.

—EVELYN WAUGH

COLLEY CIBBER

Cibber! write all thy Verses upon Glasses,
The only way to save them from our Arses.

—ALEXANDER POPE

HENRY CLAY

He was like a chameleon; he could turn any color that might be useful to him. To read of his career one must have corkscrew eyes.

—IRVING STONE

MONTGOMERY CLIFT

[He acted] like he's got a Mixmaster up his ass and doesn't want anyone to know it.

—MARLON BRANDO

Harry Cohn, movie producer

You had to stand in line to hate him.
—Hedda Hopper

(on the large turnout for Cohn's funeral in 1958)
Well, it only proved what they always say—give
the public something they want to see, and they'll
come out for it.
—Red Skelton

Samuel Taylor Coleridge

Never did I see such apparatus got ready for thinking,
and so little thought. He mounts scaffolding, pulleys,
and tackles, gathers all the tools in the neighborhood
with labor, with noise, demonstration, precept, and
sets—three bricks.
—Thomas Carlyle

Monsieur Colin

Monsieur Colin looks into ninety-eight darkened closets
and concludes from this that light is not shining outside.
—Louis Pasteur

Calvin Coolidge

I do wish he did not look as if he had been weaned on
a pickle.
—Alice Roosevelt Longworth (attrib.)

. . . simply a clean and trashy fellow, deficient in sense and almost devoid of any notion of honor—in brief, a dreadful little cad.

—H. L. MENCKEN

He slept more than any other president, whether by day or night. Nero fiddled, but Coolidge only snored.

—H. L. MENCKEN

KEVIN COSTNER

Costner has feathers in his hair and feathers in his head.
—PAULINE KAEL
(reviewing *Dances with Wolves*)

NOËL COWARD

He was once Slightly in *Peter Pan* and he has been wholly in *Peter Pan* ever since.

—KENNETH TYNAN

JOAN CRAWFORD
(after Crawford's well-received premiere of *Mildred Pierce*)

Well, none of us should be surprised. After all, my dear, you are a tradition.

—GREER GARSON

The best time I ever had with Joan Crawford was when I pushed her down the stairs in *Whatever Happened to Baby Jane.*

—BETTE DAVIS

I think she is a splendid actress, but I'm a little repulsed by her shining lips, like balloon tires in wet weather.
—JOHN BETJEMAN

SIR STAFFORD CRIPPS

There but for the grace of God, goes God.
>   —WINSTON CHURCHILL
>   (also said of Orson Welles
>   by Herman J. Mankiewicz)

OLIVER CROMWELL

That grand imposter, that loathsome hypocrite, that detestable traitor, that prodigy of nature, that opprobrium of mankind, that landscape of iniquity, that sink of sin, that compendium of baseness, who now calls himself our Protector.
>   —ANABAPTISTS' ADDRESS TO CHARLES II

MARION DAVIES AND WILLIAM RANDOLPH HEARST

> Upon my honor, I saw a Madonna
> Hanging within a niche
> Above the door
> Of the private whore
> Of the world's worst son of a bitch.
>   —DOROTHY PARKER
>   (on visiting San Simeon)

JEFFERSON DAVIS

. . . as cold as a lizard and ambitious as Lucifer.
>   —SAM HOUSTON

DORIS DAY

The only real talent Miss Day possesses is that of being absolutely sanitary: her personality untouched by human emotions, her brow unclouded by human thought, her form unsmudged by the slightest evidence of femininity.
—JOHN SIMON

Thomas E. Dewey

Dewey has thrown his diaper into the ring.
—Harold L. Ickes

[He resembled] the little man on the wedding cake.
—Alice Roosevelt Longworth

You really have to get to know Dewey to dislike him.

—James T. Patterson

Everett M. Dirksen

He has been called "the Wizard of Ooze," and a man possessed of tonsils marinated in honey.
—Ben Bagdikian

Stephen A. Douglas

As thin as the homeopathic soup that was made by boiling the shadow of a pigeon that had been starved to death.

—Abraham Lincoln
(on Douglas's ability to reason)

Theodore Dreiser

An Indiana peasant, snuffling absurdly over imbecile sentimentalities, giving a grave ear to quackeries, snorting and eye-rolling with the best of them . . . still in the transition stage between Christian Endeavor and civilization."

—H. L. MENCKEN

JOHN DRYDEN

> Ev'n copious Dryden, wanted, or forgot,
> The last and greatest Art, the Art to blot.
> —ALEXANDER POPE

MICHAEL DUKAKIS

He's the stealth candidate. . . . His campaign jets from place to place, but no issues show up on the radar screen.

—GEORGE BUSH

JOHN FOSTER DULLES

[He] stirred whiskey with a thick forefinger, his socks drooped, his suits were green-hued, his ties were indifferent, and his breath was chronically bad. Hunched forward as he talked, he droned on in a flat voice, pronouncing Anthony Eden "Ant-ny."

—WALTER ISAACSON AND EVAN THOMAS

. . . the only bull I ever knew who carried his own china shop around with him.

—WINSTON CHURCHILL

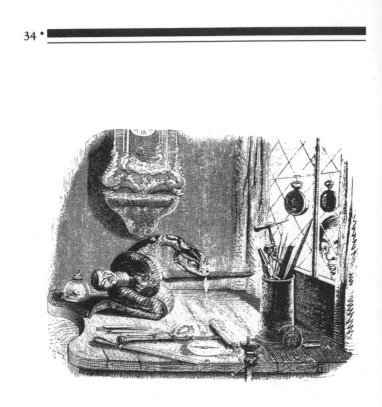

. . . a diplomatic bird of prey smelling out from afar the corpses of dead ideals.

—JAMES CAMERON

ISADORA DUNCAN

. . . a woman whose face looked as if it had been made of sugar and someone had licked it.

—GEORGE BERNARD SHAW

THOMAS EARP, English critic

> I heard a little chicken chirp:
> My name is Thomas, Thomas Earp,
> And I can neither paint nor write,
> I can only put other people right.
> —D. H. LAWRENCE

MARY BAKER EDDY

The poor woman was obviously mentally adrift from the age of five, querulous, hysterical, unscrupulous, snobbish, and almost unbelievably stupid. . . . To be a moral thief, an unblushing liar, a supreme dictator, and a cruel, self-satisfied monster, and attain, in the minds of millions, the status of a deity, is not only remarkable but a dismal reflection on the human race. She had much in common with Hitler, only no mustache.

> —NOËL COWARD

NELSON EDDY AND JEANETTE MACDONALD

Nelson Eddy and Jeanette MacDonald: The singing capon and the iron butterfly.

> —ANONYMOUS

ANTHONY EDEN

His speeches consist entirely of clichés—clichés old and new—everything from "God is love" to "Please adjust your dress before leaving."

> —WINSTON CHURCHILL

Why should I question the monkey when I can question the organ grinder?

—ANEURIN BEVAN
(interrupting his questioning of Foreign Minister
Selwyn Lloyd on seeing Anthony Eden entering the
House of Commons)

He is not only a bore, but he bores for England.
—MALCOLM MUGGERIDGE

An overripe banana, yellow outside, squishy in.
—REGINALD PAGET

Not a gentleman; dresses too well.
—BERTRAND RUSSELL

He occasionally stumbled over the truth, but hastily picked himself up and hurried on as if nothing had happened.
—WINSTON CHURCHILL

KING EDWARD VII

A corpulent voluptuary.

—RUDYARD KIPLING

DWIGHT D. EISENHOWER

I doubt very much if a man whose main literary interests were in works by Mr. Zane Grey, admirable as they may be, is particularly well equipped to be chief executive of this country, particularly where Indian Affairs are concerned.

—DEAN ACHESON

Eisenhower is the only living Unknown Soldier.
—ROBERT S. KERR

If I talk over people's heads, Ike must talk under their feet.
—ADLAI E. STEVENSON

General Eisenhower employs the three-monkeys standard of campaign morality: see no evil—if it's Republican; hear no evil—unless it is Democratic; and speak no evil—unless Senator Taft says it's all right.
—ADLAI E. STEVENSON

Why, this fellow don't know any more about politics than a pig knows about Sunday.
—HARRY S. TRUMAN

GEORGE ELIOT

George Eliot has the heart of Sappho; but the face, with the long proboscis, the protruding teeth of the Apocalyptic horse, betrayed animality.
—GEORGE MEREDITH

QUEEN ANNE, Queen of England

Anne . . . when in good humor, was meekly stupid and, when in bad humor, was sulkily stupid.
—THOMAS BABINGTON MACAULAY

QUEEN ELIZABETH I

> Oh dearest Queen
> I've never seen
> A face more like
> A soup-tureen.

—ANONYMOUS

QUEEN ELIZABETH II

Frumpish and banal.

—MALCOLM MUGGERIDGE

RALPH WALDO EMERSON

. . . a gap-toothed and hoary-headed ape, carried at first into notice on the shoulder of Carlyle, and who now in his dotage spits and chatters from a dirtier perch of his own finding and fouling: corphapheus or choragus of his Bulgarian tribe of autocophagous baboons, who make the filth they feed on.

—ALGERNON CHARLES SWINBURNE

One of the seven humbugs of Christendom.

—WILLIAM MORRIS

CHRIS EVERT

Taut and tight-lipped mistress of the baseline, she is the all-American golden girl become the champion of monotony.

—PAUL WEST

WILLIAM FAULKNER

Poor Faulkner. Does he really think big emotions come from big words?

—ERNEST HEMINGWAY

DR. JOHN FELL, Dean of Christ Church, Oxford

I do not love thee, Doctor Fell:
The reason why I cannot tell;
But this I know, and know full well:
I do not love thee, Doctor Fell.
—THOMAS BROWN

HENRY FIELDING

Fielding had as much humor perhaps as Addison, but, having no idea of grace, is perpetually disgusting.

—HORACE WALPOLE

JOHN FLAXMAN, British sculptor

I mock thee not, though I by thee am mockèd;
Thou call'st me madman, but I call thee blockhead.
—WILLIAM BLAKE

IAN FLEMING

The trouble with Ian is that he gets off with women because he can't get on with them.

—ROSAMOND LEHMANN

Stephen Fletcher, English bookseller

He was a very proud, confident, ill-natured, impudent, ignorant fellow, peevish and froward toward his wife (whom he used to beat), a great sot, and a whoring prostituted wretch, and of no credit.

—**Thomas Hearne**

Ford Madox Ford

. . . what he really is or if he is really, nobody knows now and he least of all. . . . [He is] a system of assumed personas.

—H. G. Wells

Freud Madox Fraud.

—Osbert Sitwell

So fat and Buddhistic and nasal that a dear friend described him as an animated adenoid.

—Norman Douglas

Gerald Ford

A year ago Gerald Ford was unknown throughout America. Now he's unknown throughout the world.

—Anonymous

Richard Nixon impeached himself. He gave us Gerald Ford as his revenge.

—Bella Abzug

He looks like the guy in the science fiction movie who is the first to see "the Creature."

—David Frye

In the Bob Hope Golf Classic the participation of President Gerald Ford was more than enough to remind you that the nuclear button was at one stage at the disposal

of a man who might have either pressed it by mistake
or else pressed it deliberately to obtain room service.

—CLIVE JAMES

Jerry Ford is a nice guy, but he played too much football
with his helmet off.

—LYNDON B. JOHNSON

> He can't fart and chew gum at the same time.
> —LYNDON B. JOHNSON

E. M. FORSTER

E. M. Forster never gets any further than warming the teapot. He's a rare fine hand at that. Feel this teapot. Is it not beautifully warm? Yes, but there ain't going to be no tea.

—KATHERINE MANSFIELD

BENJAMIN FRANKLIN

He is our wise prophet of chicanery, the great buffoon, the face on the penny stamp.

—WILLIAM CARLOS WILLIAMS

SIGMUND FREUD

Actually I always loathed the Viennese quack. I used to stalk him down dark alleys of thought, and now we shall never forget the sight of old, flustered Freud seeking to unlock his door with the point of his umbrella.

—VLADIMIR NABOKOV

ROBERT FROST

. . . a nice, acrid, savage, pathetic old chap.

—I. A. RICHARDS

CLARK GABLE

If you say "Hiya, Clark, how are you?" he's stuck for an answer.

—AVA GARDNER

His ears make him look like a taxicab with both doors open.

—HOWARD HUGHES

> **JOHN WESLEY GAINES (said to be a U.S. congressman)**
> John Wesley Gaines!
> John Wesley Gaines!
> Thou monumental mass of brains!
> Come in, John Wesley
> For it rains.
>
> —ANONYMOUS

JOHN KENNETH GALBRAITH

Did y'ever think, Ken, that making a speech on ee-conomics is a lot like pissing down your leg? It seems hot to you, but it never does to anyone else.

—LYNDON B. JOHNSON

JAMES A. GARFIELD

Garfield has shown that he is not possessed of the backbone of an angleworm.

—ULYSSES S. GRANT

CHARLES DE GAULLE

He is like a female llama surprised in her bath.

—WINSTON CHURCHILL

. . . a head like a banana and hips like a woman.

—HUGH DALTON

General de Gaulle is again pictured in our newspapers, looking as usual like an embattled codfish. I wish he could be filleted, and put quietly away in a refrigerator.
—SYLVIA TOWNSEND WARNER

. . . an artlessly sincere megalomaniac.
—H. G. WELLS

Boy George

Boy George is all England needs—another queen who can't dress.

—Joan Rivers

King George III

> George the Third
> Ought never to have occurred.
> One can only wonder
> At so grotesque a blunder.
> —Edmund Clerihew Bentley

King George IV

A more contemptible, cowardly, selfish, unfeeling dog does not exist than this king, on whom much flattery is constantly lavished. . . .

—C. C. Greville

> A noble, nasty course he ran,
>   Superbly filthy and fastidious;
> He was the world's "first gentleman,"
>   And made the appellation hideous.
> —Winthrop Mackworth Praed

Four Georges of England

> George the First was always reckoned
> Vile, but viler George the Second;
> And what mortal ever heard

Any good of George the Third?
When from Earth the Fourth descended
(God be praised!) the Georges ended.
                    —WALTER SAVAGE LANDOR

GEORGE GERSHWIN
George, if you had to do it over, would you fall
in love with yourself again?
                    —OSCAR LEVANT

EDWARD GIBBON

Gibbon's style is detestable; but that is not the worst
thing about him.
                    —SAMUEL TAYLOR COLERIDGE

ANDRÉ GIDE

. . . an unattractive man with a pale green complexion.
                    —SIR STEVEN RUNCIMAN

What a strange and hollow talent! Gide appears to be
completely indifferent to human nature, none of his
characters have characters, and he hangs bits of behavior
on them just as one hung different paper dresses on flat
paper mannequins.
                    —SYLVIA TOWNSEND WARNER

WILLIAM GLADSTONE, British prime minister

They told me how Mr. Gladstone read Homer for fun, which I thought served him right.

—WINSTON CHURCHILL

It was said that Mr. Gladstone could persuade most people of most things, and himself of anything.

—DEAN WILLIAM R. INGE

He has not a single redeeming defect.

—BENJAMIN DISRAELI

If Gladstone fell into the Thames it would be a misfortune. But if someone dragged him out again, it would be a calamity.

—BENJAMIN DISRAELI (attrib.)

I do not object to Gladstone's always having the ace of trumps up his sleeve, but only to his pretense that God had put it there.

—HENRY LABOUCHÈRE

[He is] really half crazy, half silly, [a man who] listens to no one and won't hear any contradiction or discussion.

—QUEEN VICTORIA

JOHN GLENN

[Senator John Glenn] couldn't electrify a fish tank if he threw a toaster in it.

—DAVE BARRY

BARRY GOLDWATER, U.S. senator and presidential candidate

I always knew the first Jewish president would be an Episcopalian.

—HARRY GOLDEN

It was hard to listen to Goldwater and realize that a man could be half Jewish and yet sometimes appear twice as dense as the normal gentile.

—I. F. STONE

MAXIM GORKY

You talk about yourself a great deal. That's why there are no distinctive characters in your writing. Your characters are all alike. You probably don't understand women; you've never depicted one successfully.

—LEO TOLSTOY
(spoken to Gorky, 1900)

LEW GRADE, BARON DELFONT OF STEPNEY, British theatrical entrepreneur
(when a knighthood was conferred on Grade, the former Louis Winogradsky)

Lord Lew Grade! Better it should be Lord Low Grade!

—ANONYMOUS

BILLY GRAHAM

Dr. Graham has, with great self-discipline, turned himself into the thinking man's Easter Bunny.

—GARRY WILLS

ULYSSES S. GRANT

The people are tired of a man who has not an idea above a horse or a cigar.

—JOSEPH BROWN

L. PATRICK GRAY III, Nominee, Director of FBI
Well, I think we ought to let him hang there. Let him twist slowly, slowly in the wind.

—JOHN D. EHRLICHMAN

THOMAS GRAY, English poet

He walked as if he had fouled his small-clothes and smelt it.

—CHRISTOPHER SMART

He was dull in company, dull in his closet, dull everywhere. He was dull in a new way, and that made many people think him *great*. He was a mechanical poet.

—SAMUEL JOHNSON

> **HORACE GREELEY**
> A self-made man who worships his creator.
> —**HENRY CLAPP**

MARVIN HAGLER, boxer

Hagler uses his bald head as a third hand. I'm a far cleaner fighter. He should be grateful I'm making him so much money. He would not get ten million bucks for fighting anyone else.

—**ROBERTO DURAN**

DOUGLAS HAIG, World War I general

. . . was brilliant to the top of his army boots.

—**DAVID LLOYD GEORGE**

JERRY HALL, actress

Try interviewing her sometime. It's like talking to a window.

—**BRYANT GUMBEL**

JOHN HANCOCK

John Hancock! A man without head and without heart—the mere shadow of a man—and yet a governor of old Massachusetts.

—**JOHN ADAMS**

Warren G. Harding

When Warren Gamaliel Harding was the twenty-ninth
president of these States in 1920, he made an inaugural
address that was described as "the most illiterate state-
ment ever made by the responsible head of a civilized
government."

—A. J. Hanna

He writes the worst English that I have ever encoun-
tered. It reminds me of a string of wet sponges; it reminds me of tattered washing on the line; it reminds me
of stale bean soup, of college yells, of dogs barking
idiotically through endless nights. It is so bad that a sort
of grandeur creeps into it. It drags itself out of a dark
abysm of pish, and crawls insanely up the topmost pin-
nacle of posh. It is rumble and bumble. It is flap and
doodle. It is balder and dash.

—H. L. Mencken

A tin-horn politician with a manner of a rural corn doctor
and the mien of a ham actor.

—H. L. Mencken

If there ever was a he-harlot, it was this same Warren
G. Harding.

—William Allen White

JEAN HARLOW

Harlow, approaching Margot, Lady Asquith, at a Hollywood party: Why, you are Margott Asquith, aren't you?

Lady Asquith: No, my dear. I am Margot Asquith. The "t" is silent, as in Harlow.

W. Averell Harriman, governor of New York

He's *thin,* boys. He's thin as piss on a hot rock.
                                    —Senator William E. Jenner

Frank Harris

Can there ever have been, since St. Paul, such a pompous, conceited, opinionated, patronizing ass? Patronizing Ruskin, Emerson, Carlyle, Whitman, Wilde, and the Prince of Wales; patronizing the Parthenon or the whole continent of North America; patronizing the arts, patronizing philosophy, patronizing God. Prose stodgy and repetitious; moralizing at once trite and windy; and as for the celebrated sex, orgasms going off as noisily and monotonously as a twenty-one-gun salute—to Frank Harris, of course.

                                              —Simon Raven

Frank Harris is invited to all the great houses in England—once.

                                              —Oscar Wilde

Jed Harris (theatrical producer)

When I die, I want to be cremated and have my ashes thrown in Jed Harris's face.

                                        —George S. Kaufman

Sandra Harris, BBC interviewer

Harris: Have English class barriers broken down?
Barbara Cartland: Of course they have, or I wouldn't
be sitting here talking to someone like you.

Bret Harte

He hadn't a sincere fiber in him. I think he was incapable
of emotion, for I think he had nothing to feel with. I think
his heart was merely a pump and had no other function.
—Mark Twain

Charles Haughey, Irish politician and occasional Taoiseach (prime minister)

If I saw Mr. Haughey buried at midnight at a crossroads,
with a stake driven through his heart—politically speaking—I should continue to wear a clove of garlic round
my neck, just in case.
—Conor Cruise O'Brien

Nathaniel Hawthorne

Hawthorne—the half man of genius who never could
carry out an idea or work it through to the full result. . . .
—Algernon Charles Swinburne

Edward Heath

In any civilized country Heath would have been left
hanging upside down on a petrol pump years ago.
—Auberon Waugh

LILLIAN HELLMAN
Every word she writes is a lie, including *and* and *the*.

—MARY MCCARTHY

Ernest Hemingway

He has never been known to use a word that might send
the reader to a dictionary.

—William Faulkner

When his cock wouldn't stand up he blew his head off.
He sold himself a line of bullshit and he bought it.

—Germaine Greer

Tommy Henrich

The most overrated underrated player in baseball.

—Larry Ritter

King Henry VIII

. . . a pig, an ass, a dunghill, the spawn of an adder, a
basilisk, a lying buffoon, a mad fool with a frothy mouth.

—Martin Luther

Katharine Hepburn

She has a face that belongs to the sea and the wind, with
large rocking-horse nostrils and teeth that you just know
bite an apple every day.

—Cecil Beaton

She has a cheekbone like a death's head allied to a manner as sinister and aggressive as crossbones.

—JAMES AGATE

She ran the whole gamut of the emotions from A to B.

—DOROTHY PARKER

ADOLF HITLER

A combination of initiative, perfidy, and epilepsy.
—LEON TROTSKY

. . . this bloodthirsty guttersnipe.
—WINSTON CHURCHILL

He is formless, almost faceless, a man whose countenance is a caricature, a man whose framework seems cartilaginous without bones. He is inconsequent and voluble, ill-poised, insecure. He is the very prototype of the Little Man. . . .
—DOROTHY THOMPSON

SIR SAMUEL HOARE, British foreign secretary

No more coals to Newcastle, no more Hoares to Paris.
—KING GEORGE V

J. EDGAR HOOVER

. . . J. Edgar Hoover, whom you should trust as much as you would a rattlesnake with a silencer on its rattle.
—DEAN ACHESON

A mythical person first thought up by the *Reader's Digest.*
—ART BUCHWALD

> I'd much rather have that fellow inside my tent pissing out, than outside my tent pissing in.
> —LYNDON B. JOHNSON

SIR GEOFFREY HOWE, member of the British cabinet

That part of his speech was rather like being savaged by a dead sheep.

—DENIS HEALEY

HUBERT H. HUMPHREY

A treacherous gutless old ward-heeler who should be put in a bottle and sent out with the Japanese current.
—HUNTER S. THOMPSON

Hubert Humphrey talks so fast that listening to him is like trying to read *Playboy* magazine with your wife turning the pages.

—BARRY GOLDWATER

ANDREW JACKSON

A barbarian who could not write a sentence of grammar and hardly could spell his own name.

—JOHN QUINCY ADAMS

GLENDA JACKSON

I watched *The Music Lovers*. One can't really blame Tchaikovsky for preferring boys. Anyone might become

a homosexualist who had once seen Glenda Jackson naked.

—AUBERON WAUGH
Private Eye, 1981

. . . an actress of some talent, whose entire persona, however, is made up of contempt and even hatred for the audience. In almost every play or film she inflicts her naked body on us, which, considering its quality, is the supreme insult flung at the spectators.

—JOHN SIMON

REGGIE JACKSON AND GEORGE STEINBRENNER

One's a born liar, the other's convicted.

—BILLY MARTIN

MICK JAGGER

He moves like a parody between a majorette girl and Fred Astaire.

—TRUMAN CAPOTE

Mick Jagger has big lips. I saw him suck an egg out of a chicken. He can play a tuba from both ends. This man has got childbearing lips.

—JOAN RIVERS

EDWARD JAMES (Wimbledon tennis umpire)

I am not having points taken off me by an incompetent old fool. You are the pits of the world.

—JOHN MCENROE

HENRY JAMES

He talked as if every sentence had been carefully re-hearsed; every semicolon, every comma, was in exactly

the right place, and his rounded periods dropped on the floor and bounced about like tiny rubber balls.

—ALFRED SUTRO

The work of Henry James has always seemed divisible by a simple dynastic arrangement into three reigns: James I, James II, and the Old Pretender.

—PHILIP GUEDALLA

I have just read a long novel by Henry James. Much of it made me think of the priest condemned for a long space to confess nuns.

—JOHN BUTLER YEATS

. . . it's not that he "bites off more than he can chaw," but he chaws more than he bites off.

—CLOVER ADAMS (Mrs. Henry Adams)

ROBINSON JEFFERS

What an ass that man is! Him and his Pacific Ocean!

—LOUISE BOGAN

THOMAS JEFFERSON

The moral character of Jefferson was repulsive. Continually puling about liberty, equality, and the degrading curse of slavery, he brought his own children to the hammer, and made money of his debaucheries.

—THOMAS HAMILTON

JESUS

No one ever made more trouble than the "gentle Jesus meek and mild."

—JAMES M. GILLIS

A parish demagogue.

—PERCY BYSSHE SHELLEY

JOSEPH JOFFRE, French marshal

The only time in his life he ever put up a fight was when we asked him for his resignation.

—GEORGES CLEMENCEAU

AUGUSTUS JOHN

Who is this chap? He drinks, he's dirty and I know there are women in the background.

—LORD MONTGOMERY

ANDREW JOHNSON

Johnson is an insolent drunken brute in comparison with which Caligula's horse was respectable.

—CHARLES SUMNER

LYNDON B. JOHNSON

... one of the few politicians with whom I found it uncomfortable to be in the same room. Johnson exuded a brutal lust for power which I found most disagreeable.... He boasted acting on the principle "Give me a man's balls, and his heart and mind will follow."

—DENIS HEALEY

When Johnson wanted to persuade you of something you really felt as if a St. Bernard had licked your face for an hour.

—BENJAMIN C. BRADLEE

When Stuart Rosenberg, the director, was called down to Washington to teach Lyndon Baines Johnson some television manners, he wailed, "How does one tell the president of the United States to stop picking his nose and lifting a leg to fart in front of the camera and using "chickenshit" in every other sentence?"

—STUART ROSENBERG

> Hey, hey, LBJ, how many kids did you kill today?
> —VIETNAM WAR PROTESTERS' CHANT

SAMUEL JOHNSON

The more one learns of Johnson, the more preposterous assemblage he appears of strong sense, of the lowest bigotry and prejudices, of pride, brutality, fretfulness, and vanity; and Boswell is the ape of most of his faults, without a pose of his sense. It is the story of a mountebank and his zany.

—HORACE WALPOLE

BEN JONSON

Reading him is like wading through glue.
—ALFRED, LORD TENNYSON

JAMES JOYCE

I could not write the words Mr. Joyce uses: my prudish hands would refuse to form the letters.

—GEORGE BERNARD SHAW

> My God, what a clumsy olla podrida James Joyce is! Nothing but old fags and cabbage stumps of quotations from the Bible and the rest stewed in the juice of deliberate, journalistic dirty-mindedness.
> —D. H. LAWRENCE

Probably Joyce thinks that because he prints all the dirty
little words he is a great novelist.

—GEORGE MOORE

An essentially private man who wished his total indif-
ference to public notice to be universally recognized.

—TOM STOPPARD

Carl Jung

Jung's latter-day philosophy, with its esoteric archtripe, fitted wonderfully with the Nazi endeavor to befuddle people's minds, make them mistrust the evidence of their own senses, and obey an elite with pure blood and impure motives.

—Dr. Frederic Wertham

John Junor, political columnist, London Sunday *Express*

The truth is, and I am not sorry to say it, Junor is a shit: a curmudgeonly old man whose taste has been for gossip, and whose stock in trade has long been the public abuse of both public and private people.

—Julian Critchley
(Conservative MP)

Elaine Kaufman, restaurateur

I flee to Elaine's a few blocks away. It is a haunt of the Mailers, the Bacalls, and the Cavetts, who know that if they are gaped at or addressed by a member of the great unwashed, the miscreant will at once be taken outside and shot. The owner, Elaine, is notorious as a lady who sits spiking bills and glares with undiluted loathing at her clientele.

—Hugh Leonard

Patrick Kavanagh, Irish poet

Mr. Kavanagh's mind, when he abandons poetry and fiction, is like a monkey-house at feeding time.

—Hubert Butler

John Keats

Why don't they review and praise *Solomon's Guide to Health*? It is better sense and as much poetry as Johnny Keats.

—George Gordon, Lord Byron

Of all the praises of that little dirty blackguard Keats, I shall observe as Johnson did when Sheridan the actor got a pension: "What! Has *he* got a pension? Then it is time I should give up *mine!*"

—George Gordon, Lord Byron

Here is Johnny Keats' piss-a-bed poetry. . . . No more Keats, I entreat. . . . There is no bearing the driveling idiotism of the Mankin.

—George Gordon, Lord Byron

Such writing is mental masturbation—he is always fr-gg–g his *Imagination*. I don't mean he is *indecent,* but viciously soliciting his own ideas into a state, which is neither poetry nor anything else but a Bedlam vision produced by raw pork and opium.

—George Gordon, Lord Byron

EDWARD F. KENNEDY

Every country should have at least one King Farouk.
—GORE VIDAL

JACK KEROUAC
That's not writing, that's typing.
—TRUMAN CAPOTE

Don King, fight promoter

Don King doesn't care about black or white. He just cares about green.

—Larry Holmes

Neil Kinnock, British Labour Leader

[He has] the consistency of the chameleon and the wisdom of the weathercock.

—Michael Howard, British politician

Rudyard Kipling

Kipling *is* a jingo imperialist, he *is* morally insensitive and aesthetically disgusting.

—George Orwell

Edward I. Koch, New York City mayor

Ed Koch is like Richard Nixon. He is forever rearranging his Enemies List in his mind. Mr. Koch is a practitioner of political sadomasochism: inflicting pain gives him pleasure.

—Jack Newfield

Judith Krantz (on her book *Princess Daisy*)

As a work of art it has the same status as a long conversation between two not very bright drunks.

—Clive James

FIORELLO LA GUARDIA

Anyone who extends to him the right hand of fellowship is in danger of losing a couple of fingers.

—ALVA JOHNSON

BONNIE LANGFORD, child actor

If they'd stuffed the child's head up the horse's arse, they would have solved two problems at once.

—NOËL COWARD
(when a horse defecated onstage)

Charles Laughton

A disappointed narcissist.

—Simon Callow

T. E. Lawrence

If he hides in a quarry he puts red flags all round.

—George Bernard Shaw

He's always backing into the limelight.

—Gerald Tyrwhitt-Wilson,
Lord Berners

JOHN LENNON

He could be a manoeuvering swine, which no one ever realized.

—PAUL McCARTNEY

OSCAR LEVANT

There is absolutely nothing wrong with him that a miracle can't fix.

—ALEXANDER WOOLLCOTT

JOHN L. LEWIS

I wouldn't appoint him dogcatcher.

—HARRY S TRUMAN

(To which Mr. Lewis replied, "The president could ill afford to have more brains in the dog department than in the Department of State.")

SINCLAIR LEWIS

Red will drink and Dorothy will talk until they both go meshuggah. . . .

—H. L. MENCKEN
(on the marriage of Sinclair Lewis and Dorothy Thompson)

ABRAHAM LINCOLN

An enemy of the human race, and deserves the execration of all mankind.

—ROBERT TOOMBS

JOHN V. LINDSAY, New York City mayor

You are nothing but a juvenile, a lightweight, and a pipsqueak. You have to grow up.

—MICHAEL J. QUILL, transit boss

Franz Liszt

Liszt's bombast is bad; it is very bad; in fact there is only one thing worse in his music, and that is his affected and false simplicity. It was said of George Sand that she had a habit of speaking and writing concerning chastity in such terms that the very word became impure; so it is with the simplicity of Liszt.

—Philip Hale

Edward Livingston, secretary of state

He is a man of splendid abilities, but utterly corrupt. Like rotten mackerel by moonlight, he shines and stinks.

—John Randolph of Roanoke

David Lloyd George

He could not see a belt without hitting below it.

—Margot Asquith

He did not seem to care which way he traveled, providing he was in the driver's seat.

—Lord Beaverbrook

Ah, si je pouvais pisser comme il parle!
(Oh, if I could piss the way he speaks!)

—Georges Clemenceau

Huey Long

[Long is] suffering from halitosis of the intellect. That's presuming Emperor Long has intellect.

—Harold L. Ickes

SOPHIA LOREN

Working with her was like being bombed by water-melons.

—ALAN LADD

CLARE BOOTHE LUCE AND DOROTHY PARKER
(both simultaneously at the door of nightclub)
Luce: Age before beauty.
Parker: And pearls before swine.

HENRY LUCE

Mr. Luce is like a man that owns a shoe store and buys all the shoes to fit himself. Then he expects other people to buy them.

—EARL LONG

MARTIN LUTHER

Luther was the foulest of monsters.

—POPE GREGORY XV

DOUGLAS MACARTHUR

MacArthur is the type of man who thinks that when he gets to heaven, God will step down from His great white throne and bow him into His vacated seat.

—HAROLD L. ICKES

THOMAS BABINGTON MACAULAY

No person ever knew so much that was so little to the purpose.

—RALPH WALDO EMERSON

He not only overflowed with learning, but stood in the slop.

—THOMAS CARLYLE

Ramsey MacDonald

I remember, when I was a child, being taken to the celebrated Barnum's Circus, which contained an exhibition of freaks and monstrosities; but the exhibit on the program which I most desired to see was the one described as "the Boneless Wonder." My parents judged that the spectacle would be too revolting and demoralizing for my youthful eyes, and I have waited fifty years to see the Boneless Wonder sitting on the Treasury Bench.

—Winston Churchill

Sit down, man. You're a bloody tragedy.
—James Maxton
(during MacDonald's last speech to the House of Commons)

He had sufficient conscience to bother him, but not sufficient to keep him straight.
—David Lloyd George

Joseph McCarthy

. . . a sadistic bum from Wisconsin.
—Hank Greenspun

Joseph McCarthy is the only major politican in the country who can be labeled "liar" without fear of libel.
—Joseph Alsop

The policeman and the trashman may call me Alice. You cannot.

—ALICE ROOSEVELT LONGWORTH
(when Senator McCarthy called her Alice)

PAUL MCCARTNEY

Paul McCartney . . . has become the oldest living cute boy in the world.

—ANNA QUINDLEN

Robert R. McCormick

The great, overgrown lummox of a Colonel McCormick, mediocre in ability, less than average in brains and a damn physical coward in spite of his size, sitting in the tower of the *Tribune* building with his guards protecting him while he squirts sewage . . . at men whom he happens to dislike.

—Harold L. Ickes

John McEnroe

McEnroe was especially irascible, and shouted assorted unprintables thirteen different times before earning another on-court audience with the referee. Lady Diana Spencer left the Royal Box during the match. "The wedding's off," someone said. "Her ears are no longer virgin."

—*Sports Illustrated*

McEnroe was as charming as always, which means that he was as charming as a dead mouse in a loaf of bread.

—Clive James

William McKinley

McKinley has no more backbone than a chocolate éclair.

—Theodore Roosevelt

HAROLD MACMILLAN

Greater love hath no man than this, that he lay down his friends for his life.

—JEREMY THORPE
(on Prime Minister Harold Macmillan's 1962 cabinet massacre)

Norman Mailer

Mailer . . . decocts matters of the first philosophical magnitude from an examination of his own ordure, and I am not talking about his books.

—William F. Buckley, Jr.

Jayne Mansfield

Dramatic art, in her opinion, is knowing how to fill a sweater.

—Bette Davis

George C. Marshall

. . . an errand boy, a front man, a stooge, or a conspirator for this administration's crazy assortment of collectivist cutthroat crackpots and Communist fellow-traveling appeasers.

—Senator William E. Jenner

Bob Martinez, governor of Florida

[Governor Martinez] exudes the warm personal charm of a millipede.

—Dave Barry

Marx Brothers

Working for the Marx brothers was not unlike being chained to a galley car and lashed at ten-minute intervals.

—S. J. Perelman

GROUCHO MARX

The man was a major comedian, which is to say that he had the compassion of an icicle, the effrontery of a carnival shill, and the generosity of a pawnbroker.

—S. J. PERELMAN

VICTOR MATURE

I never go to movies where the hero's tits are bigger than the heroine's.

—GROUCHO MARX

H. L. MENCKEN

Mr. Mencken did not degenerate from an ape, but an ass. And in the process of "revolution" the tail was eliminated, the ears became shorter, and the hind parts smaller; but the ability to bray was increased, intensified, amplified, and otherwise assified about one million times.

—J. B. TEDDER

Mr. Mencken's prose sounds like large stones being thrown into a dump-cart.

—ROBERT LITTELL

If he and the pusillanimous curs who are backing him are right, then Judas Iscariot should be sainted, and an American shrine should be erected to the memory of Benedict Arnold.

—L. L. HAYDEN

The world's greatest alphabetical montebank, perpetually suffering from logomachitis, or acute inflammation
of the stylus. If all he writes is true, he is a very sick
man.

—*CHICAGO STEP-LADDER*

He edited a magazine called *The Smart Set,* which is like
calling Cape Kennedy "Lovers' Lane."

—BEN HECHT

GEORGE MEREDITH

As a writer he has mastered everything except language: as a novelist he can do everything except tell a story: as an artist he is everything except articulate.

—OSCAR WILDE

VALERIA MESSALINA, wife of Emperor Claudius

Unfaithful bitch! Messalina! Medusa! Gorgon!

—CLAUDIUS

MICHAEL MILKEN, junk bond king

The ultimate insight of Michael Milken was that there is no limit to greed, no shackles on avarice, no end to cupidity, and that there is a seemingly endless supply of crooks and suckers.

—MAXWELL NEWTON

JOHN MILTON

Milton, madam, was a genius that could cut a Colossus from a rock; but he could not carve heads upon cherry-stones.

—SAMUEL JOHNSON

WALTER F. MONDALE

Walter Mondale has all the charisma of a speed bump.

—WILL DURST

MARILYN MONROE

Can't act . . . Voice like a tight squeak . . . Utterly un-
sure of herself . . . Unable even to take refuge in her
own insignificance.

——COLUMBIA STUDIOS (about 1948)

She was good at playing abstract confusion in the same
way that a midget is good at being short.

—CLIVE JAMES

She has no charm, delicacy, or taste. She's just an ar-
rogant little tail-twitcher who's learned to throw sex in
your face.

—NUNNALLY JOHNSON

A vacuum with nipples.

—OTTO PREMINGER

Marilyn was terribly mean. The meanest woman I ever
met in this town. I have never met anybody as mean as
Marilyn Monroe or as utterly fabulous on the screen,
and that includes Garbo.

—BILLY WILDER

**BERNARD MONTGOMERY, British Field
Marshal**
In defeat unbeatable, in victory unbearable.

—WINSTON CHURCHILL

GEORGE MOORE

> Elegy on Any Lady
> by G. M.
> That she adored me as the most
> Adorable of males

> I think I may securely boast . . .
> Dead women tell no tales.
>> —MAX BEERBOHM

> He leads his readers to the latrine and locks them in.
>> —OSCAR WILDE

CHRISTOPHER MORLEY

> He got mellow before he got ripe.
>> —CARL VAN DOREN

LOUIS MOUNTBATTEN, First Earl Mountbatten of Burma

> Dickie, you're so crooked that if you swallowed a nail you'd shit a corkscrew.
>> —GERALD TEMPLER

WOLFGANG AMADEUS MOZART

> Far too noisy, my dear Mozart. Far too many notes.
>> —ARCHDUKE FERDINAND
>> (after the first performance of *The Marriage of Figaro*)

MALCOLM MUGGERIDGE

> Malcolm Muggeridge, a garden gnome expelled from Eden, has come to rest as a gargoyle brooding over a derelict cathedral.
>> —KENNETH TYNAN

RUPERT MURDOCH

The man's charm is *lethal*. One minute he's swimming along with a smile, then snap! There's blood in the water. Your head's gone.

—JOHN BARRY
London *Times* editor

JOHN MIDDLETON MURRY

His very frankness is a falsity. In fact it seems falser than his insincerity.

—KATHERINE MANSFIELD
(Murry's wife)

VLADIMIR NABOKOV

Mr. Nabokov is in the habit of introducing any job of this kind which he undertakes by the announcement that he is unique and incomparable and that everybody else who has attempted it is an oaf and ignoramus, usually with the implication that he is also a low-class person and a ridiculous personality.

—EDMUND WILSON

GUIDO NADZO, Italian actor

Guido Nadzo is nadzo guido.

—GEORGE S. KAUFMAN

JOHN HENRY NEWMAN

. . . how odious Newman was! . . . chock-full of egotism, self-importance, self-pity, self-concern, the most tedious aspects of femininity—a real stinker, I should say.

—RUPERT HART-DAVIS

BEVERLEY NICHOLS, English writer and aesthete

A nervous wreck . . . a mercenary, hypochondriacal, flibbertigibbet who doesn't take in one of the six words addressed to him.

—EVELYN WAUGH

Richard M. Nixon

When Nixon is alone in a room, is there anyone there?
—Gloria Steinem

He told us he was going to take crime out of the streets.
He did. He took it into the damn White House.
—Reverend Ralph D. Abernathy

Nixon is a purposeless man, but I have great faith in his cowardice.
—Jimmy Breslin

If he had an affair while in office, I misjudged him. I thought he was just doing that to the rest of the country.
—John Gavin

You have to scrape diligently at Mr. Nixon's skin to find a value, traditional or otherwise.
—Howard Fast

Avoid all needle drugs—the only dope worth shooting is Richard Nixon.
—Abbie Hoffman

Richard Nixon is a kamikaze pilot who kept apologizing for the attack.
—Mary McGrory

President Nixon says presidents can do almost anything, and President Nixon has done many things that nobody would have thought of doing.

—GOLDA MEIR

The election of 1972 simply goes to prove that America is a land where the lowest common man can become president. And he did.

—KIRKPATRICK SALE

Richard Nixon means never having to say you're sorry.

—WILFRID SHEED

Nixon without his sanctimony is a man half-dressed. . . . The film of Watergate is one of our most fascinating national documents, and it will still be playing when *Gone With the Wind* has finally up and done so; and always Nixon will be there, caught with the goods and not knowing what he's done wrong.

—WILFRID SHEED

Richard Nixon is a no-good lying bastard. He can lie out of both sides of his mouth at the same time, and even if he caught himself telling the truth, he'd lie just to keep his hand in.

—HARRY S TRUMAN

He is the kind of politician who could cut down a redwood tree and then mount the stump to make a speech for conservation.

—ADLAI E. STEVENSON

He not only doesn't give a damn about the people; he doesn't know how to tell the truth. I don't think the son of a bitch knows the difference between telling the truth and lying.

—HARRY S TRUMAN

CHRISTOPHER NORTH, British literary critic

To Christopher North
You did late review my lays,

Crusty Christopher;
You did mingle blame and praise,
  Rusty Christopher.

When I learnt from whom it came,
  I forgave you all the blame,
    Musty Christopher;
I could not forgive the praise,
    Fusty Christopher.
                    —ALFRED, LORD TENNYSON

GEORGE ORWELL

He would not blow his nose without moralizing on conditions in the handkerchief industry.
                    —CYRIL CONNOLLY

MARIE OSMOND

She's so pure Moses couldn't part her knees.
                    —JOAN RIVERS

HARRISON GRAY OTIS, publisher of the *Los Angeles Times*

In the city of San Francisco we have drunk to the very dregs of infamy; we have had vile officials; we have had rotten newspapers. But we have nothing so vile, nothing so low, nothing so debased, nothing so infamous in San Francisco as Harrison Gray Otis. He sits there in senile dementia, with gangrened heart and rotting brain, grimacing at every reform, chattering impotently at all things that are decent, frothing, fuming, violently gibbering, going down to his grave in snarling infamy.

—HIRAM JOHNSON

PETER O'TOOLE

. . . there was the case of Peter O'Toole in *Macbeth,* which was so catastrophic that a departing first-nighter was heard to remark to his wife, "I'll bet the dog got sick in the car."

—HUGH LEONARD

WILFRED OWEN

Wilfred Owen's tiny corpus is perhaps the most overrated poetry in the twentieth century.

—CRAIG RAINE

THOMAS PAINE

Like Judas he will be remembered by posterity; men will learn to express all that is base, malignant, treacherous, unnatural, and blasphemous by the single monosyllable—Paine.

—WILLIAM COBBETT

WILLIAM S. PALEY

He looks like a man who has just swallowed an entire human being.

—TRUMAN CAPOTE

LILLI PALMER and CLAUDETTE COLBERT

. . . I have never—with the possible exception of Claudette Colbert—worked with such a stupid bitch.
—NOËL COWARD

DOROTHY PARKER

. . . a combination of Little Nell and Lady Macbeth.
—ALEXANDER WOOLLCOTT

NORMAN VINCENT PEALE

I find Paul appealing, but Peale appalling.
—ADLAI E. STEVENSON

DREW PEARSON, American political columnist

Pearson is an infamous liar, a revolting liar, a liar of living, a liar in the daytime, a liar in the nighttime, a dishonest, ignorant, corrupt and groveling crook.
—SENATOR KENNETH McKELLAR

He is not a sonofabitch. He is only a filthy brain child, conceived in ruthlessness, and dedicated to the proposition that Judas Iscariot was a piker.
—SENATOR WILLIAM E. JENNER

ROBERT PEEL, British prime minister

Peel's smile was like the silver plate on a coffin.
—DANIEL O'CONNELL

WESTBROOK PEGLER

Westbrook Pegler, a guttersnipe, is a gentleman compared to you. You can take that as more of an insult than a reflection on your ancestry.
—HARRY S TRUMAN
(to music critic Paul Hume, protesting review of his daughter's recital)

PERELMAN, S. J.

From the moment I picked up your book until I laid it down I was convulsed with laughter. Some day I intend reading it.

—GROUCHO MARX
(on Perelman's first book, *Dawn Ginsbergh's Revenge*)

AMBROSE PHILLIPS, eighteenth-century British poet

> Namby-Pamby's doubly mild,
> Once a man and twice a child . . .
> Now he pumps his little wits
> All by little tiny bits.
>
> —HENRY CAREY

POPE PIUS XII

You get the impression this is another dirty wop, an organ grinder.

—W. H. AUDEN

RAYMOND POINCARÉ, president of France

This devil of a man is the opposite of Briand: the latter knows nothing, and understands everything; the other knows everything, and understands nothing.

—GEORGES CLEMENCEAU

ALEXANDER POPE

There are two ways of disliking poetry: one way is to dislike it, the other is to read Pope.

—OSCAR WILDE

JOHN POPE-HENNESSY, British Museum curator

. . . that a man so bereft of human experience, who has never seen a child born or, one assumes, a woman naked (shades of Ruskin), should be considered an authority on those masterpieces of Western art that celebrate the most impassioned and most mysterious of human experiences.

—J. G. BALLARD

ELVIS PRESLEY

Mr. Presley has no discernible singing ability. His specialty is rhythm songs, which he renders in an undistinguished whine; his phrasing, if it can be called that, consists of the stereotyped variations that go with a beginner's aria in a bathtub. For the ear, he is an unutterable bore. . . .

—JACK GOULD

J. DANFORTH QUAYLE

. . . the choice of an utter nincompoop as vice president is absolute insurance against impeachment to end with J. Danforth Quayle.

MICHAEL M. THOMAS

SIR WALTER RALEIGH

I want words sufficient to express thy viperous Treason. . . . There never lived a viler viper on the face of the earth than thou.

—SIR EDWARD COKE

RONALD REAGAN

. . . the most widely beloved American since E.T.
—ROY BLOUNT, JR.

Ronald Reagan doesn't dye his hair—he's just prematurely orange.

—GERALD FORD

One hesitates even to speculate about the polyester levels of his outfits. . . . The dyed hair is . . . an outrage, as is the rouge on the cheeks. (Will the president soon proceed to eye shadow and liner?)

—PAUL FUSSELL

He is the first man for twenty years to make the presidency a part-time job, a means of filling up a few of the otherwise blank days of retirement.

—SIMON HOGGART

In a disastrous fire in President Reagan's library both books were destroyed. And the real tragedy is that he hadn't finished coloring one.

—JONATHAN HUNT

He has achieved a political breakthrough—the Teflon-coated presidency. He sees to it that nothing sticks to him.
—PATRICIA SCHROEDER

When you meet the president, you ask yourself, "How did it ever occur to anybody that he should be governor, much less president?"

—HENRY A. KISSINGER

Naming a national forest after Ronald Reagan is like naming a day-care center after W. C. Fields.

—BOB HATTOY
(Spokesperson for the Sierra Club, commenting upon a proposal to rename California's Angeles National Forest)

The battle for the mind of Ronald Reagan was like trench warfare in World War I: never have so many fought so hard for such barren terrain.

—PEGGY NOONAN, former presidential speechwriter

I know for a fact that Mr. Reagan is not clear about the difference between the Medici and Gucci. He knows that Nancy wears one.

—GORE VIDAL

I still think Nancy does most of his talking; you'll notice that she never drinks water when Ronnie speaks.

—ROBIN WILLIAMS

> . . . a triumph of the embalmer's art.
>
> —GORE VIDAL

RONALD REAGAN and MARGARET THATCHER

That most dangerous duo, President Ray-Gun and the plutonium blonde, Margaret Thatcher.

—ARTHUR SCARGILL

ROBERT REDFORD

. . . his hair is coordinated with his teeth.

—PAULINE KAEL

THOMAS B. REED, Republican Speaker of the House

He does what he likes, without consulting the administration, which he detests, or his followers, whom he despises.

—CECIL SPRING-RICE, British diplomat

WALTER REUTHER, U.S. labor leader

You are like a nightingale. It closes its eyes when it sings and sees nothing and hears nobody but itself.

—NIKITA KHRUSHCHEV

CECIL RHODES

I admire him, I frankly confess it; and when his time comes I shall buy a piece of the rope for a keepsake.

—MARK TWAIN

FRANK RICH AND JOHN SIMON

Frank Rich and John Simon are the syphilis and gonorrhea of the theater.

—DAVID MAMET

JAMES WHITCOMB RILEY

. . . the unctuous, overcheerful, word-mouthing, flabby-faced citizen who condescendingly tells Providence, in flowery and well-rounded periods, where to get off.

—HEWLETT HOWLAND

Geraldo Rivera

If Geraldo Rivera is the first journalist in space, NASA
can test the effect of weightlessness on weightlessness.
—Anonymous (in the *Chicago Tribune*)

WILL ROGERS

This bosom friend of senators and congressmen was about as daring as an early Shirley Temple movie.
—JAMES THURBER

FRANKLIN D. ROOSEVELT

I have always found him an amusing fellow, but I would not employ him, except for reasons of personal friendship, as a geek in a common carnival.
—MURRAY KEMPTON

He had every quality that morons esteem in their heroes. He was the first American to penetrate to the real depths of vulgar stupidity.
—H. L. MENCKEN

. . . a chameleon on plaid.
—HERBERT HOOVER

If he became convinced tomorrow that coming out for cannibalism would get him the votes he so sorely needs, he would begin fattening a missionary in the White House backyard come Wednesday.
—H. L. MENCKEN

Roosevelt wasn't a bump on a pickle compared to what I'd have been in the White House.
—HUEY P. LONG (attrib.)

> One-third sap, two-thirds Eleanor.
> —ALICE ROOSEVELT LONGWORTH

THEODORE ROOSEVELT

His idea of getting hold of the right end of the stick is to snatch it from the hands of somebody who is using it effectively, and to hit him over the head with it.

—GEORGE BERNARD SHAW

. . . a dangerous and ominous jingo.

—HENRY JAMES

. . . the mere monstrous embodiment of unprecedented resounding noise.

—HENRY JAMES

Theodore Roosevelt was an old maid with testosterone poisoning.

—PATRICIA O'TOOLE

JOHN RUSKIN

. . . a life passed among pictures makes not a painter— else the policeman in the National Gallery might assert himself. As well allege that he who lives in a library must needs die a poet. Let not Mr. Ruskin flatter himself that more education makes the difference between himself and the policeman when both stand gazing in the Gallery.

—JAMES MCNEILL WHISTLER

BERTRAND RUSSELL

The next time anyone asks you, "What is Bertrand Russell's philosophy?" the correct answer is, "What year, please?"

—SIDNEY HOOK

JOHN RUSSELL, British MP and prime minister

If a traveler were informed that such a man was leader of the House of Commons, he may well begin to comprehend how the Egyptians worshiped an insect.

—BENJAMIN DISRAELI

VITA SACKVILLE-WEST

She looked like Lady Chatterley above the waist and the gamekeeper below.

—CYRIL CONNOLLY

J. D. SALINGER

The greatest mind ever to stay in prep school.

—NORMAN MAILER

SIR HERBERT SAMUEL, British politician
When they circumcised Herbert Samuel, they threw away the wrong part.

—DAVID LLOYD GEORGE

Earl of Sandwich

To John Wilkes (eighteenth-century politician): Sir, you
will die either of the pox or on the gallows.
Wilkes: That depends on whether I embrace your mistress or your principles.

MADAME MARIE DE SÉVIGNÉ

You can gain nothing by reading her. It is like eating snowballs, with which one can surfeit one's self without satisfying the stomach.

—NAPOLEON BONAPARTE

THOMAS SHADWELL, seventeenth-century British dramatist

> Some beams of wit on other souls may fall,
> Strike through and make a lucid interval.
> But Shadwell's genuine night admits no ray,
> His rising fogs prevail upon the day.
>
> —JOHN DRYDEN

WILLIAM SHAKESPEARE

The undisputed fame enjoyed by Shakespeare as a writer . . . is, like every other lie, a great evil.

—LEO TOLSTOY

There is an upstart crow beautified with feathers. That with his tyger's heart wrapt in a player's hide, supposes he is as well able to bombast out a blank verse as the best of you; and being an absolute Johannes Factotum, is, in his own conceit, the only Shakescene in a country."

—ROBERT GREENE, sixteenth-century playwright

A sycophant, a flatterer, a breaker of marriage vows, a whining and inconstant person.

—EBENEZER FORSYTH

I am more easily bored with Shakespeare and have suffered more ghastly evenings with Shakespeare than with any other dramatist I know.

—PETER BROOK

With the single exception of Homer, there is no eminent writer, not even Sir Walter Scott, whom I can despise so entirely as I despise Shakespeare when I measure my mind against his. It would be positively a relief to me to dig him up and throw stones at him.

—GEORGE BERNARD SHAW

GEORGE BERNARD SHAW

George Bernard Shaw, most poisonous of all the poisonous haters of England; despiser, distorter, and denier of the plain truths whereby men live; topsy-turvy perverter of all human relationships; a menace to ordered social thought and ordered social life; irresponsible braggart, blaring self-trumpeter; idol of opaque intellectuals and thwarted females; calculus of contrariwise; flibberti-gibbet pope of chaos; portent and epitome of this generation's moral and spiritual disorder.

—HENRY ARTHUR JONES

I remember coming across him at the Grand Canyon and finding him peevish, refusing to admire it or even look at it properly. He was jealous.

—J. B. PRIESTLEY

Bernard Shaw had discovered himself and gave ungrudgingly of his discovery to the world.

—H. H. MUNRO (SAKI)

Concerning no subject would Shaw be deterred by the minor accident of total ignorance from penning a definitive opinion.
—ROGER SCRUTON

The way Bernard Shaw believes in himself is very refreshing in these atheistic days when so many people believe in no God at all.
—ISRAEL ZANGWILL

Bernard Shaw is an excellent man; he has not an enemy in the world, and none of his friends like him.
—OSCAR WILDE

NORMA SHEARER

A face unclouded by thought.
—LILLIAN HELLMAN

PERCY BYSSHE SHELLEY

A poor creature, who has said or done nothing worth a serious man taking the trouble of remembering.
—THOMAS CARLYLE

Shelley should not be read, but inhaled through a gas pipe.
—LIONEL TRILLING

THOMAS SHERIDAN, actor

Why, sir, Sherry is dull, naturally dull; but it must have taken him a great deal of pains to become what we now see him. Such excess of stupidity, sir, is not in nature.
—SAMUEL JOHNSON

CLEMENT SHORTER, British writer

There is nothing whatever to be said for Clement Shorter, a snuffling, go-getting louse in the locks of literature.

—RUPERT HART-DAVIS

CARLY SIMON

If a horse could sing in a monotone, the horse would sound like Carly Simon, only a horse wouldn't rhyme "yacht," "apricot," and "gavotte."

—ROBERT CHRISTGAU

JOHN SIMON

His warp is worse than his woof.

—BILL COLE

EDITH SITWELL

Isn't she a poisonous thing of a woman, lying, concealing, flipping, plagiarizing, misquoting, and being as clever a crooked literary publicist as ever?

—DYLAN THOMAS

I am fairly unrepentant about her poetry. I really think that three quarters of it is gibberish. However, I must crush down these thoughts, otherwise the dove of peace will shit on me.

—NOËL COWARD

KATE SMITH, radio star

Are you going to tell me how to make an entrance, you big fat tub of shit?

—TALLULAH BANKHEAD
(When hostess Smith on her radio show suggested that Bankhead count to three after walking on stage)

DAME ETHEL SMYTH, British composer

It's bad if they don't perform your [Smyth's] operas—
but when they do, it's far worse.

—CAMILLE SAINTE-SAËNS

C. P. SNOW

He doesn't know what he means and doesn't know he
doesn't know.

—F. R. LEAVIS

SOCRATES

The more I read him, the less I wonder that they poi-
soned him.

—THOMAS BABINGTON MACAULAY

ROBERT SOUTHEY

He had sung against all battles, and again
   In their praise and glory; he had call'd
Reviewing "the ungentle craft," and then
   Became as base a critic as e'er crawled—
Fed, paid, and prospered by the very men
   By whom his muse and morals had been maul'd.
He had written much blank verse, and blanker prose,
   And more of both than anybody knows.

—GEORGE GORDON, LORD BYRON
(The Vision of Judgment)

HERBERT SPENCER

The most unending ass in Christendom.
                                    —THOMAS CARLYLE

STEPHEN SPENDER

To watch him fumbling with our rich and delicate English language is like seeing a Sèvres vase in the hands of a chimpanzee.
                                    —EVELYN WAUGH

ARIANNA STASSINOPOULOS

So boring you fell asleep halfway through her name.
—ALAN BENNETT

GERTRUDE STEIN

Gertrude Stein's prose-song is a cold, black suet-pudding. We can represent it as a cold suet-roll of fabulously reptilian length. Cut it at any point, it is the same thing; the same heavy, sticky, opaque mass all through, and all along. . . .
—PERCY WYNDHAM LEWIS

Miss Stein was a past master in making nothing happen very slowly.
—CLIFTON FADIMAN

GERTRUDE STEIN, SIR JACOB EPSTEIN, and ALBERT EINSTEIN

There's a wonderful family called Stein,
There's Gert and there's Ep and there's Ein;
Gert's poems are punk,
Ep's statues are junk
And no one can understand Ein.
—ANONYMOUS

GEORGE STEINBRENNER

Do you know when George Steinbrenner is lying? When you see his lips move.
—JERRY REINSDORF

LAURENCE STERNE

. . . has that terrible, professional, nonstop pedantry of the Irish. One feels, sometimes, that one has been cornered by some brilliant Irish drunk, one whose mind is incurably suggestible.

—V. S. PRITCHETT

WALLACE STEVENS

Not-quite-Milton, a sort of origami Milton, the paper phoenix fluttering in the wizard's hand.

—HUGH KENNER

WALLACE STEVENS AND ROBERT FROST

Stevens: The trouble with you is you write about things.
Frost: The trouble with you is you write about bric-a-brac.

BARBRA STREISAND

Quite aside from her persona . . . I find Miss Streisand's looks repellent. Perhaps this is my limitation, but I cannot accept a romantic heroine who is both knock-kneed and ankleless (maybe one of those things, but not both!), short-waisted and shapeless, scrag-toothed and with a horse face centering on a nose that looks like Brancusi's Rooster cast in liverwurst. . . . Streisand remains arrogantly, exultantly ugly.

—JOHN SIMON

BARBRA STREISAND (and PAULINE KAEL and REX REED)

. . . she is undoubtedly a great inspiration to the legions of unsightly women whose banner she has carried to the heights of stardom and critical adulation that extends from Pauline Kael all the way to Rex Reed.

—JOHN SIMON

JACQUELINE SUSANN

She looks like a truck driver in drag.
—TRUMAN CAPOTE

For the reader who has put away comic books, but isn't ready yet for editorials in the *Daily News*.
—GLORIA STEINEM

JONATHAN SWIFT

Dean Swift, by his lordship's own account, was so intoxicated with the love of flattery, he sought it amongst the lowest of people and the silliest of women; and was never so well pleased with any companions as those that worshiped him, while he insulted them.
—LADY MARY WORTLEY MONTAGU

ALGERNON CHARLES SWINBURNE

I have no wish to know anyone sitting in a sewer and adding to it.
—THOMAS CARYLE

CHARLES-MAURICE DE TALLEYRAND

He is a silk stocking filled with dung.
—NAPOLEON BONAPARTE

Eugene Talmadge, Governor of Georgia

[He's] looking more like a rat than any other human being I know. . . . [with] all the mean, poisonous, and treacherous characteristics of that rodent.

—Harold L. Ickes

Elizabeth Taylor

At thirty-four she is an extremely beautiful woman, lavishly endowed by nature with a few flaws in the masterpiece: she has an insipid double chin, her legs are too short, and she has a slight potbelly. She has a wonderful bosom, though.

—Richard Burton

Norman Tebitt, Chairman, British Conservative party

A semi-house-trained polecat.

—Michael Foot

Alfred, Lord Tennyson

. . . a dirty man with opium-glazed eyes and rat-taily hair.

—Lady Frederick Cavendish

To think of him dribbling his powerful intellect through the gimlet holes of poetry!

—Thomas Carlyle

MARGARET THATCHER

She has been beastly to the Bank of England, has demanded that the BBC "set its house in order," and tends to believe the worst of the Foreign and Commonwealth Offices. She cannot see an institution without hitting it with her handbag.

—JULIAN CRITCHLEY

She ate a television journalist for breakfast and, feeling peckish, bit off some reporters' heads at a press conference.

—TREVOR FISHLOCK

Attila the Hen.

—CLEMENT FREUD

She only went to Venice because somebody told her she could walk down the middle of the street.

—NEIL KINNOCK
(when the PM attended a meeting there in 1987)

She sounded like the book of Revelation read out over a railway public address system by a headmistress of a certain age wearing calico knickers.

—CLIVE JAMES
(on a TV appearance by Margaret Thatcher)

She's the best man in England.

—RONALD REAGAN

When I hear the prime minister feeling sorry for the rest of the world, I understand why she has taken to calling herself "we"—it is less lonely.

—NEIL KINNOCK

But that will not be terribly convincing as long as the broomstick is ridden by the prime minister.

—NEIL KINNOCK, referring to the newly appointed chancellor of the exchequer "wielding a new broom"

This woman is headstrong, obstinate, and dangerously self-opinionated.

—PERSONNEL OFFICER AT ICI
(in a report rejecting Margaret Thatcher for a job)

I cannot bring myself to vote for a woman who has been voice-trained to speak to me as though my dog has just died.

—KEITH WATERHOUSE (attrib.)

If I were married to her, I'd be sure to have dinner ready when she got home.

—GEORGE P. SHULTZ

DYLAN THOMAS

That insolent little ruffian, that crapulous lout.
When he quitted a sofa, he left behind him a smear.
My wife says he even tried to paw her about.

—NORMAN CAMERON
Excerpt from poem "The Dirty Little Accuser"

Thomas was an outstandingly unpleasant man, one who cheated and stole from his friends and peed on their carpets.

—KINGSLEY AMIS

He was cartilaginous, out of humanity, the Disembodied Gland, which was my coinage; Ditch, which was Norman

Cameron's; the Ugly Suckling, which was Bernard Spencer's, indicating a wilful and at times nasty babyishness.

—GEOFFREY GRIGSON

DOROTHY THOMPSON

She is the only woman who had her menopause in public and got paid for it.

—ALICE ROOSEVELT LONGWORTH

I just had dinner with Dorothy Thompson and her husband, whom I'd never met before. I began by thinking how awful they were, but ended by deciding they were not so bad—though she is so ignorant and so silly that one wonders why anybody has ever let her go into print about politics and he is one of those all-too-heavy jolly Viennese lightweights.

—EDMUND WILSON

Ignorant bitch. Shrieking hurricane. . . . Poor Red Lewis, stuck with that.

—H. L. MENCKEN

J. R. R. TOLKIEN
(during the reading of a Tolkien manuscript)

"Oh fuck, not another elf!"

—HUGO DYSON

HERBERT BEERBOHM TREE

Do you know how they're going to decide the Shakespeare-Bacon dispute? They are going to dig up Shakespeare and dig up Bacon; they are going to set their coffins side by side, and they are going to get Tree to recite *Hamlet* to them. And the one who turns in his coffin will be the author of the play.

—W. S. GILBERT

ANTHONY TROLLOPE

Trollope! Did anybody bear a name that predicted a style more Trollopy?

—GEORGE MOORE

HARRY S TRUMAN

The president would lick any Jewish arse that promised him a hundred votes.

—ERNEST BEVAN

I don't care how the thing is explained. It defies all common sense to send that roughneck ward politician back to the White House.

—SENATOR ROBERT TAFT

DONALD TRUMP

The Prince of Swine.

—MICHAEL M. THOMAS

Mark Twain

. . . a hack writer who would not have been considered fourth rate in Europe, who tricked out a few of the old proven "surefire" literary skeletons with sufficient local color to intrigue the superficial and the lazy.

—William Faulkner

George Villiers, second duke of Buckingham

> Stiff in his opinions, always in the wrong;
> Was everything by starts, and nothing long;
> But in the course of one revolving moon,
> Was chymist, fiddler, statesman, and buffoon.
> —John Dryden

Richard Wagner

Listening to Wagner's music, every musically healthy person gets a terrible *Lamentum Katzarum,* that is, *Katzenjammer.*

—Isaak Moses Hersch

The prelude to *Tristan und Isolde* reminds me of the Italian painting of the martyr whose intestines are slowly being unwound from his body on a reel.

—Eduard Hanslick

Wagner was a monster. He was anti-Semitic on Mondays and vegetarian on Tuesdays. On Wednesday he was in favor of annexing Newfoundland, Thursday he wanted to sink Venice, and Friday he wanted to blow up the pope.

—Tony Palmer

Wagner, thank the fates, is no hypocrite. He says out what he means, and he usually means something nasty.

—James Gibbons Huneker

Is Wagner actually a man? Is he not rather a disease?
Everything he touches falls ill: he has made music sick.
—FRIEDRICH WILHELM NIETZSCHE

Wagner's music is better than it sounds.

—MARK TWAIN

Richard Wagner, not only a composer but regarded by
some, for his libretti, as one of the great poets of his
era. He was also a crook, a hypocrite, a poseur, and a
spiteful, hysterical bigot.

—ANTHONY HECHT

Wagner has beautiful moments, but awful quarter
hours.

—GIOACCHINO ROSSINI

MRS. HUMPHREY WARD

. . . that shapeless mass of meaningless flesh—all old and
sordid and insignificant.

—LYTTON STRACHEY

ANDY WARHOL

He is the only genius with an IQ of 60.

—GORE VIDAL

> **JACK WARNER, Hollywood movie producer**
> He has oilcloth pockets so he can steal soup.
> —WILSON MIZENER

JAMES G. WATT, U.S. secretary of the interior

The Secretary has gone bonkers. It's time the white-coat people took him away.
—SENATOR GAYLORD NELSON

EVELYN WAUGH

He looked, I decided, like a letter delivered to the wrong address.
—MALCOLM MUGGERIDGE

GOTTFRIED WEBER, German music critic

Oh, you arch-ass—you double-barreled ass!
—LUDWIG VAN BEETHOVEN

DANIEL WEBSTER

The word "honor" in the mouth of Mr. Webster is like the word "love" in the mouth of a whore.
—RALPH WALDO EMERSON

. . . the most meanly and foolishly treacherous man I ever heard of.
—JAMES RUSSELL LOWELL

Mae West

If I possessed the power of conveying unlimited sexual attraction through the potency of my voice, I would not be reduced to accepting a miserable pittance from the BBC for interviewing a faded female in a damp basement.

—GILBERT HARDING
(on being asked to sound more sexy
interviewing Mae West)

EDITH WHARTON

She is always *pitying* workers; poor things, how they do have to work!

—LOUISE BOGAN

JAMES MCNEILL WHISTLER

I have seen, and heard, much of Cockney impudence before now; but never expected to hear a coxcomb ask two hundred guineas for flinging a pot of paint in the public's face.

—JOHN RUSKIN
(After this remark Whistler sued for slander, and won—one farthing.)

With our James vulgarity begins at home.

—OSCAR WILDE

WALT WHITMAN

As to his originality in the matter of free speaking, it need only be observed that no remarkable mental gift is requisite to qualify man or woman for membership of a sect mentioned by Dr. Johnson—the Adamites, who believed in the virtue of public nudity.

—ALGERNON CHARLES SWINBURNE

He was a vagabond, a reprobate rake, and his poems contain outbursts of erotomania so artlessly shameless that their parallel in literature could hardly be found with the author's name attached.

—MAX NORDAU

Under the dirty clumsy paws of a harper whose plectrum is a muck-rake, any tune will become a chaos of discords. . . . Mr. Whitman's Eve is a drunken apple-woman, indecently sprawling in the slush and garbage of the gutter amid the rotten refuse of her overturned fruit-stall: but Mr. Whitman's Venus is a Hottentot wench under the influence of cantharides and adulterated rum.

—ALGERNON CHARLES SWINBURNE

OSCAR WILDE

When Oscar came to join his God,
Not earth to earth, but sod to sod,
It was for sinners such as this
Hell was created bottomless.

—ALGERNON CHARLES SWINBURNE

What a tiresome, affected sod.

—NOËL COWARD

BILLY WILDER

His critiques of films are subtle and can be very amusing, especially of the ones he hasn't seen.

—DAVID HOCKNEY

KING WILLIAM III

He's ugly and crooked,
His nose it is hooked,
The Devil to him is a beauty,

Nor father nor mother
Nor sister nor brother
Can ever bring him to his duty.
                    —ANONYMOUS (circa 1688)

Ralph Vaughan Williams

Listening to the Fifth Symphony of Ralph Vaughan Williams is like staring at a cow for forty-five minutes.

—Aaron Copland

Harold Wilson, British prime minister

He had no sense of direction, and rarely looked more than a few months ahead. His short-term opportunism, allied with a capacity for self-delusion which made Walter Mitty appear unimaginative, often plunged the government into chaos. Worse still, when things went wrong he imagined everyone was conspiring against him.

—Denis Healey

He is going round the country stirring up apathy.

—William Whitelaw

If he ever went to school without any boots it was because he was too big for them.

—Ivor Bulmer-Thomas

Sloan Wilson and Herman Wouk

If the Man in the Gray Flannel Suit married Marjorie Morningstar on my front porch at high noon, I wouldn't bother to go to the wedding.

—Nelson Algren

TOM WOLFE

. . . the nonchalant master of the neon-piped sentence.
—HUGH KENNER

MARY WOLLSTONECRAFT

A philosophizing serpent . . . that hyena in petticoats.
—HORACE WALPOLE

ALEXANDER WOOLLCOTT

He looked like something that had gotten loose from
Macy's Thanksgiving Day parade.

—HARPO MARX

. . . a butterfly in heat.

—LOUIS UNTERMEYER

Reply to Alexander Woollcott's boast—"What is so rare
as a Woollcott first edition?"
"A Woollcott second edition."
—FRANKLIN PIERCE ADAMS

VIRGINIA WOOLF

V. Woolf's "A Writer's Diary": usually done in "fifteen
minutes before dinner." What a monster of egotism she
was!

—LOUISE BOGAN

Virginia Woolf's writing is no more than glamorous knitting. I believe she must have a pattern somewhere.

—EDITH SITWELL

She had been a peculiar kind of snob without really belonging to a social group with whom to be snobbish.

—EDMUND WILSON

WILLIAM WORDSWORTH

In his youth Wordsworth sympathized with the French Revolution, went to France, wrote good poetry, and had a natural daughter. At this period, he was a "bad" man. Then he became "good," abandoned his daughter, adopted correct principles, and wrote bad poetry.

—BERTRAND RUSSELL

Mr. Wordsworth, a stupid man, with a decided gift for portraying nature in vignette, never yet ruined anyone's morals, unless, perhaps, he has driven some susceptible persons to crime in a very fury of boredom.

—EZRA POUND

He keeps one eye on a daffodil and the other on a canal-share.

—WALTER SAVAGE LANDOR

One finds also a kind of *sincerity* in his speech. But for prolixity, thinness, endless dilution, it excels all other speech I had heard from mortals. A genuine man, which is much, but also essentially a small genuine man.

—THOMAS CARLYLE

YEVGENY YEVTUSHENKO

. . . a ham actor, not a poet.

—ALLEN TATE

ISRAEL ZANGWILL, British author

He is an old bore; even the grave yawns for him.

—HERBERT BEERBOHM TREE

Author Index